Maurice Thompson

My First Voyage

and other Stories

Maurice Thompson

My First Voyage
and other Stories

ISBN/EAN: 9783743305458

Manufactured in Europe, USA, Canada, Australia, Japa

Cover: Foto ©ninafisch / pixelio.de

Manufactured and distributed by brebook publishing software (www.brebook.com)

Maurice Thompson

My First Voyage

MY FIRST VOYAGE.

I.

WHEN I was a boy my father had a government contract that took him to the little town of Bay St. Louis, which is built on the high western shore of a beautiful bay of the same name, on the gulf coast of Mississippi. I was the only child my father had and, my mother being dead, I was petted and spoiled a good deal by well-meaning people wherever I went. At Bay St. Louis, where we were living during the two years that my father's contract lasted, I was allowed to run free for a great part of the time. I fished a good deal, wandered in the grand forests of pine, oak and magnolia that stretched indefinitely away east of the town, and, indeed, did just as I pleased. My father was a very busy, industrious man, grimly intent upon retrieving a lost fortune, and I think he never dreamed that I was possessed of anything like an imagination. At all events the only books he left in my way were tables of logarithms, sines and tangents, treatises upon earthwork, timber structures, jetties, breakwaters and the like, together with two or three volumes of chemistry and geology. So you may imagine with what ravenous avidity I attacked Robinson Crusoe when I got the chance. A traveller left the book, a well-worn paper-covered copy, at our boarding-house and thus it came to my hands. I devoured it, as a hungry animal devours food, in an ecstasy of delight.

No doubt Robinson Crusoe is a very charming book and quite harmless in a general way, but it caused me the most serious trouble I have ever experienced, so far as personal suffering is concerned.

I read and re-read the story, until its spirit got full possession of me, and then I began to long for an adventure of my own. Day after day, when my father was absent in pursuit of his undertaking, I sat upon the breezy bluff and gazed out on the blue water of the beautiful bay, dreaming of some day going away in a ship and getting wrecked on a tropical island where I could live an ideal Crusoe life.

An old negro man, with whom I became well acquainted, added a great deal to my foolish desire by telling me romantic stories of pirates and smugglers whose ships, he said, were all the time hovering just beyond some little marsh islands, barely visible on the southern horizon when the weather was very favorable.

I grew so interested at length that I thought of nothing else but the imaginary delights of a lonely life on some far-away, undiscovered shore. I dreamed of it throughout my sleep and pondered over it every hour of the day.

My father was a practical, rather austere man and I did not mention my fanciful ambition to him; but to Uncle Luben, the old negro, I told everything. Of course the kind-hearted, ready-tongued African, thinking I was merely giving vent to a boyish imagination, entered fully into the spirit of all my plans.

"'F I's you I'd des rig up one o' dem leetle boats down yer at de landin', an' I des sail erway some o' dese yer moon-shiny nights, dat w'at I'd do," he said in his wise, solemn way. "Kase dey's mo' oranges, an' figs, an' grapes, an' watermellions, an' bananers on dem fur-off islands 'an eber you see in all yer bo'n days, chile. Dey's cantaloups bigger 'n a flou' bar'l an' cocoanuts 'at you couldn't hardly tote, an' den de honey, w'y de honey it des grow on de bushes down da'."

I don't know that I believed all that Uncle Luben told me, but there was the blue bay spreading away to the far horizon where La Fitte the pirate used to sail, and just off yonder in the southeast, was the Caribbean Sea, where the Buccaneers so long found a safe home. I felt the fascination of the balmy salt breezes and the spell of the semi-tropics was upon me.

"Uncle Luben," I said to the old negro one day, "I have got my plans all made. I'm going on a voyage to-night. You'll never see me again."

"Dat's it, child, dat's des it!" he responded, shaking his white woolly head approvingly. "Now you's a talkin' sense. Go right 'long an' see de big ocean an' de water-mellion islands an' de cocoanut trees an' all. Lawsy me ef I's young like you I'd des turn in an' go clean all eround this worl', I tell you!"

Well, that night, sure enough, I departed on my voyage of adventure. You need not fear that I am going to tell you a dream. It is a genuine experience and it has a good enough lesson in it, I think. However, I must hasten to add that I don't believe boys nowadays ought to need any lesson of the sort.

It was a splendidly beautiful moonlight night in May, warm, balmy, exhilarating. A gentle breeze was blowing seaward. The little town of Bay St. Louis was still and peaceful as it slept along the high tree-shaded bluff — a town in fact one house deep and nine miles long.

Near midnight I crept out of my bedroom window with a little bundle under my arm. My father was soundly sleeping. The whole world seemed to be wrapped in a deep, solemn dream.

I felt that I was not doing quite right; in fact I

knew I was doing wrong, but the sea was calling me, the great, mysterious, shining sea, and I could not resist.

Down to the landing I went with my bundle under my arm and waded out to my father's little boat, which lay anchored in the shallow water. I knew a little about sailing, just enough to render me confident, but not enough to give me command of the boat in any, save the most favorable weather. My father would not have permitted me to go out alone under any circumstances.

Hastily but silently I pulled up the little anchor and set the sail as best I could. The boat was a mere skiff, but staunch and good, rigged with a shoulder-of-mutton sail, a centre-board and a rudder. Fortunately the wind was not strong, and it blew steadily southward, so that I got the little craft before it and sailed away without much trouble. Little I dreamed of the danger I was about to encounter as I looked back and saw the shining white line of the town slowly receding as the wind bore me along. I shall never forget how wondrously blue the sky was, and how the stars, despite the great brilliancy of the moon, flared and flashed, like the flames of candles shaking in a wind. A weatherwise person would have known that a storm was gathering not far off, for there was a peculiar dampness and freshness in the air, and an ominous film hung about the horizon. But I sailed on, all unconscious of the indications and wrapped in the fascination of my escapade.

A flock of pelicans, their wings shining in the moonlight, flew ahead of me for a while, keeping just above the little waves. They appeared to be leading me on toward a low fringe-like marsh-island just beginning to be visible in the far south.

Now the breeze stiffened a little, giving my boat an impulse which caused white whisps of spray to flash about the gunwales. A thrill seemed to run over the wide waste of water and little white-capped waves leaped and murmured all around me. A sudden sense of loneliness filled my mind and involuntarily I glanced back. A strange mist had enveloped the shore. A broad booming sound arose, as if from the depth of the distant parts of the sea. I felt my heart sink. Strangely enough, I thought of the soft, sweet bed in the cosey room and of my father sleeping so soundly after his day's work. Just then a big bird, flying wildly before the wind, passed overhead with a hoarse scream; then a cloud covered the moon.

I was thoroughly frightened and made a great effort to turn the boat about and go back; but the breeze was now lifting the water into foaming billows and I saw how powerless I was.

When one's conscience is not just right one is a coward. I lost my head and went into a state of hysterical ecstasy, throwing my arms about and screaming as loudly as I could. It was as if the wind grew hysterical too, for now it howled and raved and leaped upon my boat, whirling it about and driving it before it like a straw or a dry leaf. I had to let go the tiller and cling to the gunwales, as the little vessel leaped and tumbled with the ever increasing waves. My hat blew off and went whirling away into the boiling, foaming water. Then the storm struck in earnest and I felt the sea spring up, like a giant, to show its real strength.

I PEEPED OVER THE TOP OF THE GRASS.

Something happened, I do not know what, for I was buried in the water.

II.

I have said that this is no dream-story, but I really felt as one feels who opens his eyes after the most horrible visions of sleep. I looked about, as best I could, and saw nothing but tall marsh grass and weeds. I was lying almost face-downward in a slimy place where the mud looked black and nasty. My head roared, my limbs ached, my hair and mouth were full of slime; and at first I could not imagine what this all meant. After many trials I rolled myself over and managed to get up on one elbow and gaze all around. Then I looked at myself. My clothes were soaked with water and covered with mud. Was this a dream? At first I was inclined to think it was, but very soon I knew it was not, for I began to recollect the circumstances and incidents of my voyage. Slowly it dawned upon me that I was indeed a lonely shipwrecked boy on a desolate marsh. Painfully I dragged myself into a sitting posture only to find that my head was so dizzy and sore that I could scarcely hold it up.

The sun was about an hour high in what I thought was the east, and I judged that it was early morning, which proved to be so. I dragged myself out of the muddy place and lay down on the rushes and weeds. The sky was clear now, the wind, very gently blowing out of the southeast, was as sweet as May and the sea could make it, and the sunshine was very soothing to my chilled and bruised body and limbs. I lay there on my back and gazed up into the blue heaven thinking over my predicament with a forlorn consciousness of how wicked I had been.

At length I thought of trying to look about for my boat. Possibly it had been cast up on the shore somewhere; and if I could find it I might make my way back to my home. I was on the point of making an effort to get upon my feet when I heard a voice, heavy and peremptory in its tone, say

"Set the box down here, Jim, it will be safe enough for the present, and we will go look for the most favorable point on this island. I think it'll suit our purpose."

"All right, sir," said another voice.

"Well, come on now," added the first, "we've no time to lose."

The first thought that sprang into my mind was that these men were smugglers. I lifted my head cautiously and peeped over the grass. They had deposited a small red box on the ground and were now walking away across the island. I saw that the box had bright bands of brass around it. Uncle Luben had told me a great deal about strong boxes of gold and other treasure often buried by these lawless men.

I was very much frightened now when I thought of the probability that these men would discover me, and kill me, perhaps, for fear that I might disclose some of their secrets.

When the sound of their voices had died away in the distance as they walked off, I peeped over the top of the grass again and took a good view of the surroundings. At a little distance from the box a boat, about the size of the one I had got wrecked in, but much more beautiful, was moored to the shore, its sail flapping lazily.

As I sat there looking first at the box and then at the boat and dreading the return of the men, a great desire to get away from the island took possession of me, and then, with a jump of my heart, I thought of capturing the smugglers' boat and escaping in it. Why not? There it lay ready for me; and the owners were out of sight. It did not take me long to decide. Every moment was precious.

I crawled down to the edge of the water, fearing that if I stood up the men would see me, and unmoored the boat. Then I chanced to have a brilliant conceit. Why not take the box? Oh, if I could go home with a captured boat and a priceless treasure-box!

I re-tied the boat and crawled back to the box and dragged it down to the water. It was very heavy for me to handle, but I finally heaved it aboard and then I managed to get the little craft off before the wind. This is all very easy to tell and may appear tame and simple, but to me at the time it was terribly exciting. Every moment I expected the men to return and wreak their revenge upon me for my rash undertaking. A minute was like an hour. Then, too, I was so weak and sore that every move I made was torture.

When the box was safe in the bottom of the boat, and I was sitting, tiller in hand, with the sail bulging gently and the little vessel beginning to glide away from the low, marshy shore, I felt so glad and thankful that the pain and hunger were quite forgotten. Far away northward I could see the dim line which marked the bluffs of Bay St. Louis. The wind would blow me straight to my home! I turned and looked back, and as I did so a gruff voice came bellowing over the water:

"Hello, there! bring back that boat, you scamp you!"

The two men were running along the shore and making all sorts of frantic gestures. I was scared almost out of my wits, but I held a steady hand on the tiller, so that the boat kept on before the breeze.

Never, I am sure, did men cut such wild capers and yell and shriek as they did. It did them no good, however, for I sailed right on my course. I felt free and victorious. No boy of my age had ever performed so daring a thing as to capture the boat and treasure-box of pirates or smugglers.

The thought gave me renewed strength and firmness. They screamed and shouted and called me names and shook their fists at me, but on I went.

III.

Meantime, at Bay St. Louis my father and his friends had searched the town and all the country round for me, and great excitement prevailed. No one, not even Uncle Luben, thought of my attempting a voyage alone, for the old negro had taken all my talk as mere boyish prattle, and my father had never heard a word of it. True, the boat was missed, but it was supposed that the storm had loosed it from its anchorage and blown it away to sea. Several other small craft had been lost in the same way, on account of the suddenness of the gale.

It was about the middle of the afternoon when I proudly steered my captured vessel and cargo up to the landing under the tree-fringed bluff of Bay St. Louis. Some one recognized me and gave the word to others and soon a crowd gathered to see me. My father heard the outcry, and I saw him hurrying towards me, his face pale and excited.

Everybody was so glad to see me alive that great shouts went up from the men while some of the women cried. As soon as I went ashore I was surrounded and a hundred questions were asked me at once. No wonder my father looked at me so strangely, for I was muddy from head to foot, haggard, wild-eyed, my hair all matted and my clothes torn into tatters. I tried to tell my story, but somehow I could not. I pointed to the boat and the box.

"Why, that's the surveyor's boat!" cried some one, "how'd the boy get that?"

"It *is* the surveyor's boat," repeated another, "where's the surveyor?"

I felt weak and faint. My father had to carry me to the house, and for four long, weary weeks I lay on my bed sick with fever. During all that time I was wholly unconscious of the great joke the towns-people had to tease the surveyor with. As you have suspected, no doubt, it was a surveyor and his assistant whom I had taken for pirates. The brass-bound box contained a transit, which is a sort of compass with a telescope attached. Some persons who thought of locating a building on the island had sent the surveyor down there to plat it, and I had run away with his boat and instrument, leaving him and his assistant to take care of themselves as best they could!

But I paid dearly for that escapade. I suffered all the pangs of a rheumatic fever, and then, when I began to get well, I felt so much remorse for what I had done that it was long before I could look my father in the face and promise him, of my own accord, never to do such a thing again.

HOW NED SCALED MT. WASH-
INGTON.

"WELL, sir, I'm sorry, but it can't be helped. You are a little ahead of the season."

"Well — but — I say, isn't there a way of managing it — by paying double fare, or something of that sort?"

"No, sir," said the clerk; "it can't be done. The season doesn't begin until the middle of June, and it wouldn't pay the company to start running cars up the mountain until there are people to go. Come back in about four weeks and you'll find us running up, but just now you will have to content yourself with a sight of the mountains."

Ned Stanley turned from the clerk with a very disappointed face. Here he was at the White Mountains — at the far-famed Fabyan House, rested by a night's sleep and ready for the ascent of Mt. Washington. He had come all the way from Missouri — had been studying up the trip, and particularly the ascent for months. He had seen stereoscopic views of the elevated railway and had imagined himself in sundry dangerous and exciting situations. He had, in fancy, retailed the adventure to his less fortunate companions at home, unconsciously making himself, and not the railway, the central figure. He had been asked by various imaginary persons:

"Did you go up Mt. Washington?" and had answered, "Of course; the White Mountains without Mt. Washington would be like the play of Hamlet with Hamlet left out." (He had heard that from a chance acquaintance on the train and it struck him as a particularly neat and original way of putting it.)

Now to get here and be told that the cars wouldn't run for four weeks was a little too much! If anybody should ask about Mt. Washington he could only say, "The cars were not running and I couldn't go up," and then perhaps the other fellow might "quote Hamlet." Then there was Tom

Winston. He gave a pebble a vicious kick. Tom had ventured some advice because he had once been to Chicago and felt his superiority as a traveller, and Ned had said not very graciously, "Now, don't you fret, Tom, about me. I've studied this thing up and know what I'm about if I haven't been to Chicago." Of course Tom would ask about the ascent of Mt. Washington and tell the other fellows, and — oh, yes, Hamlet was left out!

The mountains were there in their majesty, 'tis true, and Ned had said to himself that morning as he saw the sun rise over Mt. Washington, "This pays a fellow for the ride" — but the glory of it was gone now.

He wandered down to the Mt. Pleasant House, back again, and up to the White Mouutain House; "anything," he said, "to kill time."

Mt. Deception, back of the hotel, looked inviting and he determined to climb that. The view was good, and had it not been that Mordecai sat at the king's gate in the shape of unattainable Mt. Washington he would have been more than satisfied with it.

Returning, he found it was time for dinner, which he prolonged as much as possible. He was strongly tempted to take an earlier train for Portland, but having planned to leave Fabyan's at four he determined to carry out the programme as far as he could.

After dinner he walked down to the station "to see the other fools get caught," he said savagely to himself. But the train puffed in and out and nobody was caught. Ned's dissatisfaction increased. It seemed that he was the only traveller who didn't know Mt. Washington's office-hours!

He tried to strike up a conversation with the agent, but found him uncommunicative and preoccupied, after the manner of agents with inexperienced travellers.

"I think I'll take a stroll to the foot of the mountain," said Ned, as the agent put his key into the door preparatory to locking up.

"I should," said the man, dryly, as he started off. "It'll give you good exercise.'

"How far is it?" asked Ned. But the man was gone.

Ned deliberated: "I can't get lost if I follow the railroad, and I can say I've been to the foot of the mountain anyway. I'll see one end if I can't the other."

He started down the track. There was a good deal to see, after all, for a boy who had never beheld a mountain, and Ned found his spirits rising as he walked.

He sauntered along, stopping now and then to break off a specimen with the geologist's hammer which he carried in his pocket, and once to make a sketch.

"I'll make a better one from it when I get home," he promised himself as he put it away and jogged on.

Mountain air is deceptive, and the distance which looked so short to Ned lengthened out to six miles before he reached the foot of the mountain.

Here the elevated railway begins. Ned crossed from one track to the other and took a look around. There was not much to see. It was unsatisfactory after his long walk.

He looked up the mountain track — it didn't look very hard to climb — and there must be something to see, even just a short way up.

He took out his watch and found, to his surprise, that it was already too late to make the four o'clock train.

And then Ned did a very foolish thing. He deliberately turned his back upon Fabyan's and started up the mountain.

Not that he had any idea of going to the top — he told himself definitely that he should only go a short distance — just far enough to get a view; and then he should retrace his steps and reach Fabyan's in time for a late supper.

The first part of the ascent was rather a disappointment. Ned had not expected to see so many trees, but had pictured the whole of Mt. Washington as being like the stereoscopic views of the top — all bowlders and lichens. More than once he turned to go back, saying to himself that it hadn't paid, but something drew him on — perhaps more a dogged determination to see something worth seeing, than anything else.

As he went on the trees grew smaller and scarce, the chasms widened and deepened, Mt. Madison and Mt. Monroe lifted their heads above the clouds, and before he knew it Ned was standing still, drinking in the glories of Mt. Washington.

There was no turning back now. He must have the view from behind yonder bowlder — once there, he must cross the trestle-work beyond and look into the chasm over which it hung.

Time, fatigue, cold, were forgotten. The one desirable thing in life, now, was to see. As I said, he was a Western boy accustomed to level prairies and sluggish streams, and this taste of mountain scenery intoxicated him.

As he pressed on beyond the shelter of the overhanging rocks a sharp wind struck him with a sudden chill. He stopped and looked back.

The track wound down the mountain side like a serpent. At the foot the shadows had deepened till he could not tell tree from track. The valley was full of gloom and a dull mist obscured objects that he had but just now noticed.

Could it be growing dark down there?

He looked up the mountain. This track was clearly defined, the western light bringing everything out in relief.

A glance at his watch turned his face homeward with a sudden sense of alarm. Where had the time gone? Would he be able to make it before dark? He certainly had not a moment to lose.

In turning to descend, Ned had the same experience we all have had, doubtless: He found it was one thing to go up a steep place and quite another to go down. Moreover, he had suffered from childhood from dizziness in looking down any steep descent. He always had hated himself for having such a womanish weakness and had suffered tortures to keep the knowledge of it from the boys; but it lurked still, ready to overpower him now at any moment.

To add to the danger of the descent there was a frost gathering on the track and increasing every minute. Ned had gone but a few steps when his foot slipped on a treacherous tie and he was thrown violently back. The grade was very steep at that point — so steep that Ned had fancied it must be

HE SET FIRE TO A PAPER AND THREW IT DOWN.

"Jacob's Ladder." As he sat holding on to the rails he looked over the trestle to see what he had escaped. One glance was enough! He drew back, sick and faint — his old enemy had him!

He sat still, with closed eyes, trying to think what he should do. He must go on — there was no alternative — but he dreaded to stand up and face that chasm below. He said to himself that he must not — he would not — grow dizzy; and of course, this very nervousness increased the dizziness.

It was a lonely plight for a boy to be in, halfway up the mountain side, not a human soul within miles, and night coming on! How fast it was coming on! At that instant the sun dropped in behind the hills, and Ned, accustomed to prairie sunsets and the long afterglow, found he had counted upon more daylight than he was likely to have.

Nerving himself for another trial, he cautiously got upon his feet. As he did so he missed his hammer which he had had in his hand when he fell. Looking around, he found it hanging in the cog-rail a few steps above him where he had probably thrown it in his efforts to catch himself. Going back for it he found, to his surprise, that it was easy enough to go up — that it was the downward motion which had produced the dizziness.

This discovery brought him to a standstill again. Since he couldn't go down, at least not without much danger, why not go up?

If this was really Jacob's Ladder he was half way up now. If he went on he should be getting more of the fading daylight all the time; if he went down into the valley he should be going from it.

Then, there was another consideration. When he got to the top he should be sure of a hot supper and a bed; if he went down there would be that long walk to Fabyan's after he reached the base. Ned's exercise had made him hungry, and the thought of ham and eggs, beefsteak and hot coffee, turned the scale in favor of the Summit House.

Having once determined to go on, he walked briskly forward, wishing to make the most of the daylight left. He looked into no more chasms, but kept his gaze on the track ahead and on the mountain tops across the ravines. He saw a tiny spark on the top of one, and, as he looked, wondering what it could be, another came, and another, and then he knew the stars were out. He had a strange feeling of companionship as they formed themselves into the familiar constellations. They were the same old stars, anyway, the same his mother was watching now, perhaps, out on the prairie. He was glad she did not know where he was.

There was no moon yet, but it would rise, he thought, before he reached the top. The starlight enabled him to see the track, but the scraggy trees and brush took strange shapes. Ned was sure once that a man stood by the track a little ahead. When he reached it it was a dwarf-spruce. Another time a horse's head rose before him as the track turned, but proved to be only a jutting rock. Ned was not conscious of fear, but he could not keep these strange shapes out of his mind.

He stepped cautiously along the ties but once a

shadow deceived him and he bore his whole weight upon that. Down he went between the ties, almost to his armpits. He drew himself up again bruised and panting. Lighting a match, he set fire to a paper and threw it down looking to see what it might light up. He found he was on a trestle, perhaps thirty feet high, and the grade was the steepest he had yet encountered.

Ned dared not trust himself, after this experience, to walk, but laying aside everything but his instinct of self-preservation he took the ties as the rounds of a ladder and continued his journey on all-fours. The ties were slippery and cold and Ned soon felt stiff from his unaccustomed position, but not knowing anything about the turns in the road he thought it better to bear these ills than to risk those he knew not of.

He never knew just how long he was in reaching the top. Chilled through and through, with hands so numb they could hardly do their work, he toiled on only because there was nothing else he could do.

At last the moon rose, and almost at the same moment a monument appeared at the right. This

Ned recognized from the pictures as the monument erected to the memory of Lizzie Bourne, who perished on this spot years ago. As ghostly as it looked in the moonlight, it sent a thrill of joy through his heart, for he knew it was only a few steps from the top. And sure enough another turn brought him out upon a level track with a platform by its side.

Ned looked around him with an interest quite natural under the circumstances. At his right was the Summit House where he expected to find the supper and the bed. To his surprise, all was dark. It must be later than he had thought.

He lost no time in finding the door and giving a sounding knock. Nothing answered but the echoes. It was strange, there was no light in the office. He wondered, as he knocked again, how they made it pay this time of the year. They must depend upon the railroad travel for custom. A horrible thought here flashed over him. Could it be that the hotel was not open?

It was even so. Ned was on the top of Mt. Washington, alone.

For a few minutes he almost gasped — from the discovery and the rarified air together. What could he do? His common sense came to the rescue. Why, get into the house, of course. He would freeze to death outside.

He scratched a match, shielding it from the wind with his hat, and examined the window to see how it was fastened. There was an ordinary catch at one side, which he could easily manage if he could get at it. By breaking one pane of glass he could do that. Stones are plentiful on the top of Mt. Washington and Ned felt no compunction in using one. The catch yielded readily to his touch and the next minute he was in the office of the Summit House.

Another match and a little search showed him a bracket lamp, and a light made the gloomy room almost cheerful. The next thing was a fire. There was a large coal stove in the middle of the room kept burning all summer for the comfort of guests, and Ned soon had a roaring fire. He could not wait for coal, but made it of wood, enjoying heartily its snap and crackle.

He held his stiffened fingers to the blaze and, as the warm shivers ran up his back and loosened his joints, thought it wasn't such a bad adventure after all.

He next took up the lamp and started on an exploring tour. But with all his lucky happenings he happened upon nothing to eat. Returning to the office he helped himself to one of the Summit House letter-heads and wrote a letter to the writer of this story, dated "Top of Mt. Washington," in which he detailed his adventure.

He found himself ready for bed early after his unusual exertions and having choice of rooms he was soon covered with warm blankets, sleeping the sleep of the — young.

He awoke bright and early the next morning and started out to make observations. He found himself on a plateau about an acre in extent. The Summit House was the largest building, but near were the old Tip Top House and the Signal Station. If Ned had only known it he might have found companions in the two officers who spend nine months of the year here alone.

But he did not know it, and being reminded by an inward craving that his breakfast hour was past and a walk of nine miles yet before him he took a farewell look and prepared to descend.

By day and in good weather the descent is not a dangerous one, and Ned found no difficulty in going rapidly ahead, sometimes walking on the track, sometimes beside it, and occasionally, where the grade was steep, riding on a board placed across the rails, using his feet as brakes when he found himself going too fast.

It was a glorious walk and paid him, he thought, for all the hardships and risks of the night before. But still it was rather a forlorn young man that presented himself before the clerk at Fabyan's that morning asking meekly if it was too late for breakfast. He told the whole story, not dwelling much upon the climbing, which, indeed, was not necessary since his trousers corroborated the story, but telling of the broken window and the stolen lodging. "I'll pay you whatever is right," he said, " if it's under your management."

The clerk smiled. " It isn't under our management exactly," he said. "I really should have no right to take the money. And then," he said, dryly, contrasting the figure before him with the stylish young man of yesterday, "I rather guess you've paid your way already, haven't you?"

And Ned rather thought he had.

THE USE OF IT.

"COME on, Joe; it's a pink of a day for a frolic in the woods. Father's started for the Station and I hid until he was off, I was so 'fraid he might leave me something extra to do. But I'm free for all day, so come on, I say!"

"Can't, Ben."

"Why not?"

"I must ride Black Harry around the pasture until he's tired and stops racing; then I'm to ride him along the road as far as the Post-office."

"Well, if you must you must," said Ben, "but I'm sorry for a feller who can't have his freedom such a glory-fine day as this. By the way, Joe, did I tell you, father's going to buy me a bicycle?"

"You don't say!"

"Yes, true as guns! Can you go to-morrow morning to the woods if it's pleasant?"

"No; got to saw wood."

"Well, I declare! What's the use of a fellow's having to hammer away at something in the way of work all the time? Vacation too!"

"I can do whatever I like all the long afternoons," said Joe a little disconsolately; "but father thinks boys ought to learn to do all sorts of useful things."

"But what's the use?" asked Ben.

"I suppose father knows; and he says I will one of these days if I live. But ain't you the lucky boy to have a bicycle!"

A whoop interrupted them and two or three other boys appeared from around the corner; bright-eyed, active-limbed and fairly dancing with fun and merriment were the new-comers as they accosted Joe and Ben in lively boy fashion:

"Come on, Toodlewigs! Hop around there, Bouncer! We're off for a berry-picking, and our noon meal in the cool shadow of the berry bushes, where we shall dig a hole and roast some 'taters, pop some corn, and have a nice little racket all to ourselves.'

"Joe can't go," said Ben, "he's got to ride his majesty, the young Black Harry, round the lot till he's all fagged out, then take him to the Post-office for the mail."

Joe laughed, but told the boys why he must remain on the place for at least two mornings.

"Well, it's too bad," said the merry boys; "but we must be off or the robins will get the berries before we arrive. Day, day, Joe, boy, a nice ride to you!"

Black Harry was a splendid young horse raised on the place; somewhat strong-headed, fleet, but yet trustworthy if judiciously handled, else Dr. Benner had hardly given orders to his only son, fourteen-year-old Joe, to ride him around the lot until he was tired. The boy had been trained to the saddle from a child. He had also been carefully instructed as to the use of axe and saw, and many other tools; also how to load and discharge a gun, to row, and manage a sail boat; and the boy was a capital swimmer.

Dr. Benner was sometimes called an eccentric man, and so perhaps he was; but those who knew the Doctor best considered him more sagacious than peculiar.

Joe's mother had died during his babyhood, and the Doctor realized as he once expressed it, that the boy would most likely be whatever by God's blessing he chose to make him, which he hoped ultimately would be a whole man; so he had set conscientiously to work for that result.

"Well done!" said the Doctor to himself, as pausing on his long round of calls he stopped for a moment at the wide pasture and peeped through the bushes.

"Well done! the boy manages his charger well and no mistake!"

Black Harry was literally tearing with leaps and bounds from one part of the pasture to the other; occasionally a little stump would threaten to impede his progress, but with a frolicsome plunge he would leave it far behind, while the sturdy young rider who sat the animal with perfect ease would now and then draw a tighter rein or speak a word of command, when the bounding creature would obey at once as if in complete sympathy with his master's wishes.

At length, after a long season of headlong speed, Black Harry put on more style, as slackening his pace he arched his long neck, and stepping high and daintily like Puss herself, at a signal from Joe, he easily leaped the low strip fence and pranced along the road in the direction of the Post-office.

Joe received the mail, and soon after stood watching his father in the study as he began examining his letters.

One missive proved to be a circular; and as Dr. Benner opened it, there appeared before Joe's longing eyes pictures of bicycles of most attractive form and style, the slender wheels seeming almost to roll and move. Joe spoke:

"Oh, father, how I do wish I could have a bicycle!"

"Well, why don't you have one, my son?"

"Are you really willing I should?" asked Joe delightedly.

"Certainly, my boy."

"And when may I get it?"

"Just as soon as you can earn it."

Joe's countenance fell. It had been a comparatively easy thing earning his money for the Fourth of July which was close at hand, as so many farmers had been glad of extra help during the early haying; but to earn the sum required to purchase a first-class bicycle — really that was too bad of his father.

"Ben Low's father is going to give him a bicycle," said Joe experimentally. "I think he's a wonderfully lucky fellow."

"Yes, I should think he was," said the Doctor without looking up from his reading.

"And Ben has all day to himself to spend as he likes," added Joe.

"When Ben gets his bicycle, you let me know how many hands high it is, will you?" said the Doctor dreamily.

"Yes, indeed I will!" Joe answered eagerly.

"And his father gives him no tasks, eh?"

"Well" — Joe hesitated — "Ben did say he hid

until his father left the house this morning, for fear he might leave him a task."

"My son!" Dr. Benner suddenly woke up, his voice ringing, his glance sharp as a needle:

"My son! if for any reason I neglect to give you a task in the morning during your vacation or at any time hereafter, and you see anything you think ought to be done, I wish to feel I can rely on you to do it. I suppose I can trust you?"

"Yes, father, I think you can, I'm sure I want you to," he added with boyish sincerity.

"Very well," was the abrupt rejoinder; "by being faithful in little things, you may in time reap large rewards — and you may not. At all events an approving conscience will be found an exceeding benefit; but don't forget when Ben Low's father buys his bicycle to let me know just how many hands high it is. I shall be interested to hear," he added dryly.

Joe was vaguely conscious that his father's tone was a little incredulous, or mocking, or something of the kind; but he could not quite divine it, and soon forgot the impression entirely.

There was to be a Convention of medical men in the city thirty miles distant on the third of July. Excursion tickets were placed within the means of all wishing to avail themselves of an opportunity to profit by the occasion. Eminent physicians from all parts of the State would meet to compare facts and experiences well worth the hearing of those interested in medical lore or surgical skill.

Dr. Benner was to leave home on Wednesday morning, the third, expecting with many others to return on the afternoon of the Fourth of July; and on the next day, the fifth, the Doctor had been planning for a long time to take Black Harry to a Cattle Show and Horse Fair, and place the beautiful animal on exhibition for the day.

This time the Doctor left no extra tasks for Joe, remarking that as he was to have a holiday trip himself, Joe might pass the time as he thought best, provided nothing unforeseen should occur to demand his attention.

Straightway the merry boys fell to planning a grand picnic to take place on the Fourth. Fire crackers and punk had been purchased in abundance at the village store. Mrs. Merriam, Dr. Benner's housekeeper, was to make biscuit, chocolate cake, frosted cake and doughnuts, the other boys providing sandwiches, boiled eggs, lemons and sugar. And Joe and his friends went to bed in good season on Wednesday night in anticipation of the next day's sport.

Thursday was bright and beautiful. Joe felt in no haste as the party was not to start very early. He ate his breakfast leisurely, then packed his basket, and having bade Mrs. Merriam a joyous "good-by," started out to meet the other boys.

He sped over the lawn in front of the house, and was darting across the pasture when a loud whinny close by caused him to stop a moment. Black Harry came slowly up, then mutely held up one hoof from which the shoe was hanging nearly off.

"Oh dear!" exclaimed Joe impatiently, "what made you show that to me now, Harry? I can't help you, old boy, indeed I can't — I can't!" he repeated despairingly as the exact situation forced itself upon him with vexing rapidity.

John, the Doctor's man, had already availed himself of Dr. Benner's permission to make a little visit on his own account, expecting to meet his master at the depot in the afternoon. The only other man, a farm hand, was not to be trusted with the romping Harry, and Joe knew only too well it would be a great disappointment to his father should anything prevent his taking the horse to the Fair early the next morning.

What could be done!

The blacksmith was two miles away, and a horse could almost never be shod short of an hour, and oftener not for two or three hours after reaching the smithy's, unless taken early in the morning, "and it'll be just the same Fourth o' July or no Fourth o' July!" said poor Joe desperately.

What could be done!

To give up the picnic and his Fourth of July — his Independence Day frolic — just for Black Harry's shoe seemed too hard to contemplate for a moment; and just then a "whoop-a-la," burst on the lad's ear and there was Ben Low and the rest of the party, baskets in hand, all ready for a start.

Instantly there flashed through Joe's mind a recollection of the decided words his father had spoken only a few days before, about relying on him to do anything he thought ought to be done whether the task was given him or not; the sight of Ben Low had seemed somehow to revive the conversation, and on the instant he also remembered his father's permission to pass his time as he thought best, provided nothing unforeseen should occur to demand his attention.

And although his father had allowed that reward might possibly attend the faithful performance of duty, Joe was too much accustomed to obeying from principle to do so from any other motive.

There was a sharp, brief conflict; then Joe turned resolutely towards his friends:

" I can't go, boys."

" Why? Why? Why, I should like to know?" cried one of his companions.

" Do not my ears deceive my eyesight!" exclaimed another tragically.

" He's mad! Great Hercules, yes! His senses

JOE FLAGS THE TRAIN.

do now forsake him!" cried a third striking a stagey attitude.

But the facts were briefly explained, and the disgusted boys finally convinced that Joe was in earnest.

Ben Low turned petulantly away with a familiar question: "Well, I say, Old Scruples, what's the use? S'pose it'll ever pay, being so awfully cons'entious?"

"Time'll tell," said Joe cheerily, and beginning to whistle to keep up heart as they all turned away.

Joe remembered that his father had said he wished whoever went next to the blacksmith's would take the hatchet and have an edge put to it. He took it from the tool-chest, then unpacked his basket, making a smaller parcel containing a good lunch, and having been duly petted and pitied by motherly Mrs. Merriam, and telling her he might not return for several hours, he soon started off, riding Black Harry carefully, that the graceful creature might not grow lame from travelling too rapidly without a shoe.

Now and then he thought with a twinge of regret of his lost holiday sport, but after a long, hot ride over the country roads and through quite a stretch of woods, he at last reached the blacksmith's where it seemed as if every fine horse for miles around was awaiting his turn to be shod.

The day would have been a trying one but for the fact that Joe, being an enterprising, intelligent lad, fond of seeing what was going on and learning something new if possible, became interested in watching the men at their work. He liked to see the fiery sparks fly from the forge; liked to see the grinding wheel go swiftly round gradually sharpening the dull edge; and there was not a little diversion in listening to the remarks and opinions of the different ones who had a horse to be shod or an axe to be ground.

At four o'clock in the afternoon Joe started for home thinking he would go around by the railroad.

One topic of conversation at the smithy's that day had attracted his attention more than any other, and had impressed him unpleasantly. Considerable had been said about the ponderously long train which was to bring the doctors home, leaving them at different towns all along the county, and how the time and signals had been arranged with great accuracy to give the Excursion train ample time to avoid the regular Express.

"Wall, I s'pose Benjamin Low ought to know what he's 'bout," said a burly countryman, "but I tell you it's resky business, this switchin' an' signallin' great crowded trains. Wants a man o' stiddy habits and clear brains to keep his wits about him, and not make any mistakes, I tell *you!*"

There was general concurrence in the man's views, and Joe noted the fact with an uneasy sensation. It seemed there must be a lurking suspicion or knowledge of possible unfaithfulness on past occasions, regarding Ben Low's father, yet he must have been considered trustworthy to be left with such great responsibility.

The switch-tender's little station was still two miles farther away from home; but mounted on Black Harry firmly shod, and impatient after standing still so long, it was the merest run.

So with the nicely sharpened hatchet across his

lap away sped Joe, and in a very short time he came unexpectedly upon the switch-tender himself lying flat by the side of the station in a heavy sleep.

In vain Joe shouted and called. The man could not or would not waken. Joe grew cold with a strange anxiety and apprehension. The place was very lonely; he had passed but a single habitation during his two miles' ride, and that about midway, fully a mile back. It would be hard work summoning aid.

Hastily slipping from Black Harry's back, he secured him, then grasping Mr. Low by the shoulder he shook him as vigorously as he could.

The sleeper roused himself a little and gazed stupidly at Joe's face.

"Is the switch all right?" called Joe.

"You — fix — switch," he mumbled.

"I say!" Joe called again, "wake up, Mr. Low, wake up, I tell you! Two loaded trains are coming along in half an hour! Are the switches attended to, and the signals all right?"

"You — see — sig'alls." Then the poor drunken

man fell flat again overcome by the fatal drowsiness.

Joe realized the exact situation and set his sharp boy's wits to work. He himself was ignorant of switches and signals. There was not a moment to lose; he must stop that incoming train. But how?

For three precious minutes he thought intently, then exclaimed excitedly, "Yes, I have it!" Springing into the saddle he put Black Harry to his utmost speed.

A mile ahead, still following the track, was a high knoll; if only he could gain that point and rig up some kind of a signal, he might warn them in time, his precious father among the rest — he *must* do it!

He reached the spot, again fastened Black Harry, then climbed wrist over wrist the first low-branched tree he came to, firmly grasping the hatchet in one hand.

"Luckiest thing in creation I happened to have this hatchet along," he said aloud, as he began chopping off a long, firm branch.

It was dexterously done and hatchet and branch

were dropped to the ground just as the Excursion train whistled at the next station beyond. In five or six minutes more she would pass the spot where Joe was waiting.

Would they see him if he remained on the ground? No; he must mount Black Harry, holding him with one hand, and his signal in the other, then trust to his horsemanship and skill in coaxing and commanding to control the mettlesome animal when the train should come thundering around.

Tearing off his checked blouse, he tied it firmly with his handkerchief to the end of the long, willowy pole, and mounting Black Harry, he waved his signal aloft as the train came with a swoop and a roar around the curve, only quarter of a mile distant.

Black Harry plunged and reared, but obeyed astonishingly the peremptory voice of his young master, as the rushing thing came on. In his excitement as the train swept by, Joe not only waved his signal wildly, but shouted at the top of his strong young voice:

"Stop! Oh stop! For Heaven's sake, stop, I

THE USE OF IT.   63

say!" Then he heard the sharp alarum whistle, saw the brakeman hastily twisting the metals, and still waving his signal high in air, he raced after the slackening train.

An hour later, when the danger was past, but fully realized, the grateful passengers from both rescued trains were forcing upon Joe's acceptance a generous gift hastily collected ; the spontaneous expression of their admiration of the boy's pluck and of their thankfulness ; but his father held him back.

The Doctor's shrewd eyes were decidedly moist as he asked for the third time in his dry, characteristic way, viewing the purse as if it were a natural curiosity :

" But what could he do with it — a lad like him who has a father ? "

" Do with it ? " roared a wealthy farmer from up country, who in company with his son, a young physician, had attended the convention ; "do with it ? Why, man alive ! let him buy peanuts with it if there is nothing else he wants more, but don't say a fellow sha'n't give a little thank-offering for the savin' o' his life and only son's, let alone there bein' several scores of us alive and whole, as might a-been crushed to atoms, but for this young hero o' yourn!"

The speech so loud at first ended in a tremble.

"Might as well give in, Doctor, for this once," said another old gentleman; "we couldn't rest in our beds to-night if the boy went unrewarded."

And the Doctor had to give in, because the people would have their way; and they went off leaving their gift in Joe's hands.

That night, after recounting the events of the day to his father, Joe added: "I suppose I can use some of my present for a bicycle, can't I?"

"No; my son," said Dr. Benner, laying his hand on Joe's knee, "no, my boy, the Bank will be the best place for that at present. I hardly approved that way of rewarding a simple act of humanity, but not wishing to wound the feelings of any one waived my own inclinations in the matter. But I shall buy you a bicycle myself in a day or two, because I think — well — I think, my boy, all things considered, you have *earned* one. You lost your holiday sport, but saved your honor as to trustworthiness.

Then he added with his occasional startling energy: "But I want to tell you one thing, my child, Benjamin Low was once before found sleeping at his post. It was a long time ago, and people began to feel assured he would not be guilty of like infidelity a second time. But if in your youth you yield to temptation of *that* kind, I doubt if in your manhood you are either loyal to duty, or possess so much as a thimbleful of pluck. And I don't believe a son of yours would own a bicycle half a hand high — remember that, my boy!

"And as to the *use* of faithfulness in little things: Well, if you had let Black Harry go without his shoe and risked disappointing me to-morrow, it is doubtful whether you and father would be talking safely and contentedly with each other to-night as we are doing — extremely doubtful, Joe."

NAN'S BAMBINO.

IT surely all came from Nan's wearing spectacles. Not stylish, saucy "nippers," but regular, gold-bowed spectacles. They made her look about ten times as knowing as any fourteen-year-old girl has any business to be. They cast a sort of distinguishing halo about her eyes. For Nan was not far-sighted; she was not near-sighted; she was not cross-eyed; nor bleared-eyed. But the trouble was *as-tig-ma-tism*, and it took an unabridged dictionary for the other girls to find out what that meant. Nan was the only young person in town with that long-worded disease, so her position was an enviable one — from a certain point of view!

Nan never forgot her dignity, nor her spectacles. She even kept them close by her bedside at night, in case of sudden illness or fire. If she happened to wake before morning (which she did about twice in the course of a year), she immediately clapped her glasses on, to see that all was right.

But this particular night, Nan was not asleep; she was sitting bolt upright in bed, spectacles on nose, straining both ears to hear the words which came through the open door.

"If we go to Europe, Nan must go too."

"Well — but — consider — "

"There's no 'but' about it, John dear. Not a step will I stir without my one chick. Neither will you. You know you would be perfectly miserable with the Atlantic Ocean between you and your girl."

"So I should. So I should," admitted "John," who was no other than Nan's father. The next moment he gave an exclamation of surprise, for, on the threshold, stood Nan, her eyes shining like two stars behind the glittering glass of her spectacles.

"O, Daddy!" she gasped, and there were volumes in those two words.

Her father laughed.

"You shall go, my little kid," he said. And go she did.

The marvels which presented themselves to those spectacles are not to be counted.

They peered at the cogs and wheels and pistons of the *Gallia's* engines. They took a survey of the "steerage" to see where Mikey McGrath and Blitsen Sneiders ate their meals and "slept the sleep" of the *comparatively* "just."

They "spiered" at Roslyn Chapel, near Edinburgh, and the like of its wondrous carvings they had never seen. They looked round all the corners in London Tower, and grew so misty in the room where the Two Little Princes were smothered, that Nan had to actually give up wearing them for several minutes.

They stared at the grandest woman that was ever made — the deathless "Venus of Milo," in the Louvre, and the busy brain behind them cried out, "Oh! Oh!! Oh!!!" and could find no other words sufficient for the occasion.

Those glasses "took in" the lovely Swiss lakes, and their owner's heart gave a great throb of delight when they saw the blessed old "Northern Dipper" shining calmly above the Alps, just as much at home among such lofty companions as when twinkling over "Stubb's Hill" in America.

And now Nan was in Rome, safely quartered in the blue-papered room at Madame Chapman's Pension, on the Via Nasionale.

Nan didn't care much for the "ruins" in Rome. She had not begun her Latin yet and knew about as much of Julius Cæsar and Cicero and the rest of those ancient worthies, as most of us do concerning Thothmes II. of Egypt, or of Heliogabalus. So the "Forum" was alas! of little consequence to those gold-bowed spectacles, and, I regret to state, that their ignorant little owner called the "Coliseum" "an old, tumble-down, brick shanty." Instead of listening to the thrilling tales of the deeds of heroism and of valor which had taken place on that spot, Nan was making friends with a group of dirty Italian children, and coaxing them to let her hold their "*bambino*" (baby) which gazed at her imperturbably with round, black, beady eyes.

In fact the Italian *bambini* were Nan's especial delight in Rome. And how they did swarm. Babies to the right, babies to the left. Babies in the stived-up back streets; babies surrounding Trajan's Forum; babies on the Bridge of St. Angelo. That was where, on this particular morning, Nan and her mother were pausing; mamma examining Bernini's "Breezy Maniacs" (great angels, with fluttering wings and garments), Nan casting hasty glances at them and then making sundry darts at one, two, three babies, by the way.

"Come, Nan, come," said her mother. "If we are going to St. Peter's this morning, we must hurry, for the rain will catch us before long."

Indeed the rain did catch them, in spite of their hastening steps. They could only rush hurriedly across the great Piazza in front of St. Peter's and take a hasty refuge in the vestibule.

How the rain came down! It pelted and it poured. The music of the fountains, in front of the church, was wholly lost in the rushing sound of the deluge from the skies.

And yet, as Nan and her mother stood gazing

out, what should appear but a group of people, walking along as complacently as if they were not dripping wet, and as if the water could not have been wrung out of a certain blue bundle which one of the party carried.

"And, mother!" cried Nan, in a great excitement, "I verily believe it's a *Baby* wrapt in blue silk, and coming, in all the storm, to be baptized!"

Before her mamma could interfere, Nan had run up to the group, her whole face aglow, her eyes beaming with sympathy behind those gold-bowed spectacles.

"*Bambino?*" she was saying eagerly. "A—h!"

Such an expressive "A—h!" those simple-hearted Romans had never heard. Never did spectacles look more solemn.

"*Bambino?*" questioned Nan.

"*Bambino!*" said one of the women, lifting a corner of the blue silk.

There it lay, that eight-days-old baby, looking as clean and as comfortable as any baby in the world.

The heavy, leathern portière, which serves for a

door, was pushed aside, and the party entered the great church. Eager Nan followed on its heels.

In the first side chapel on the left stands the enormous font. Its heavy, brazen top had been removed. Toward this chapel the baby was carried. Nan again approached. This time she held out her arms.

"*Bambino!*" she repeated imploringly, and, suddenly, to her surprise, greatly to her delight, she found herself holding that droll little baby. It was as stiff as a stick of wood, for, like many Italian babies, it was swathed tightly. Not a foot could this *bambino* move. Nan's eyes winked hard, partly with pleasure, partly with embarrassment. A tall priest, clad in gold-embroidered vestments, stood waiting at the font. One of the women attempted to take the baby. "A — h!" pleaded Nan again.

The woman showed two rows of white teeth, and, almost before she knew it, Nan found herself assisting at the baptism, in the capacity of *nurse*.

Not a word of the Latin service, excepting the

"Amens," could she understand, but she was keenly alive to her duties, and followed the guidance of the woman on her left.

The priest breathed on the baby; put salt on its little red tongue; touched its breast and back with oil; and then Nan, according to direction, held her little stiff burden out, at right angles to her own body, with its head over the font, while the water was poured on its black hair.

How it came to pass that she was allowed to do all this, I do not know. I can only tell you that no one made any objection. The gentle women smiled on her. The young father of the baby seemed quite flattered by the attention.

After all was over, Nan tried a few words in Italian. "*Americana*," she said, pointing to herself.

The women nodded.

"*La Madre — Amore*" — Nan went on.

A puzzled look came into the young father's eyes, but it gradually dawned on him that this extraordinary little individual was trying to send her love to the baby's mother.

They all shook hands in the kindest fashion.

If the women looked strange to Nan, in their coral necklaces, big gold ear-rings and striped aprons, there is no doubt that she impressed them quite as much. But hearty good-will lay at the bottom of all their sentiments. "*Grazie*" they murmured.

And "*Grazie!* Thank you ever so much! *Grazie!*" said Nan.

"Weren't they — oh! *weren't* they good to let me hold the *bambino?*" she cried to her mother, who had stood near, watching the whole affair.

Nan never saw those people again; but she often wonders how that Italian baby is getting along, and she says, "I rather think I'm the first American girl who ever played 'Nurse' in St. Peter's, Rome."

IN THE LINE OF THE EARTH-QUAKE.

IT had been the quietest night possible. Not a breath of air stirred among the gray-green olives of the hills. The Mediterranean lay like a steel-blue mirror spread out for the stars to look down on. All the world was still asleep, dreaming, if at all, of that gay Carnival time which had but just ended, and whose fantastic, unreasoning mirth-making might well pursue one into the droll land of dreams, when suddenly through the dusky stillness of the early morning there came a sound like the booming of a distant battlefield, or the breaking of an angry surf upon a long line of shore, accompanied by a trembling and jarring and rumbling of the whole earth, as when a mighty train thunders past some tiny wayside station. And then all in a moment, before I had time to question what it meant, our house began to rock violently to and fro, as if some great monster of the world below had seized upon it in his hand and was shaking it as a terrier shakes a rat. I sprang up in bed in horror, almost suffocated by the plaster dust in the air, while the war of the earthquake was drowned in the noise of shivering china and falling furniture, of straining, breaking timbers, and of tottering partitions that groaned like human things in agony as the walls were wrenched asunder. It was like looking on at what one imagines the end of the world might be — a sudden awful instant of unheralded and overwhelming destruction.

The first shock, from beginning to end, lasted less than fifty seconds, when all was still again; but in a few moments more, before I could free myself from the entanglement of bent rods and fallen curtains and masses of solid plaster (which, but for those same iron rods, bent over me like protecting arms, would indubitably have killed me on the spot), there came a second shock, shorter and far less severe than the first, but alarming enough even so, as we stood with the hanging walls and loose boards shaking and rattling around us like the flapping sails and creaking cordage of a ship in the midst of a gale.

Fortunately our stairway was still standing, for one's best chance of safety at such a time lies in escaping between the shocks to some open space out of reach of the falling buildings; and seizing whatever lay nearest to hand, we rushed down and out to a public garden, where we found a crowd of panic-stricken fugitives like ourselves, in every variety of scanty costumes, roughly cloaked in rugs and blankets snatched up in mad haste as they fled, and all with faces unforgettably white and ghastly and full of that nameles dread of those who have looked Death close in the face and have caught glimpses of things unutterable.

At first we sat or stood about in groups, awed into utter speechlessness. All sorts of odd things happened, but at the time nothing struck us as either ludicrous or surprising. One invalid, who had not walked for years, under the fright of the earthquake ran in her nightdress and bare feet from her hotel to our garden, which was some squares away, and the same curious unaccountable recovery of lost powers was reported of several paralytics who were instantaneously cured by the shock. By degrees however, as all continued quiet, confidence returned; the more venturesome made daring raids back into the houses to save what they could from the general wreckage; tongues were loosened, and strangers and friends talked indiscriminately, exchanging their various experiences and retailing many hairbreath escapes as miraculous as my own; and some broke down completely and sobbed hysterically, and others tried to laugh and make a joke of it, not realizing that their jesting seemed as out of place as merriment in a graveyard, while a child and a little dog with alert brown ears and bright eyes gleaming with frolic — the only two uncomprehending happy beings among us all — struck up an intimate friendship, and made sport with each other in and out between the frightened people, and played bo-peep over the heaps of reserved household belongings flung in motley piles upon the gravel, and were hungry and ate biscuits with undisturbed, every-day appetites.

So time wore by in wretched suspense, till three hours later a third shock came, which paralyzed laughter and sobs alike on the instant, and drove back the blood from every face, and many rushed screaming into each other's arms and frantically embraced, thinking to die together. It was horrible to look up through the clear bright sunlight and see the houses swaying and staggering like drunken things, and hear the deep, hoarse, sullen, subterranean growl, and the sound of crashing and rending and breaking on every side, followed by such a cry sent up from a whole cityful of terrified people as surely one never hears but once. And then came silence again, a silence almost worse than any sound, for in it one heard one's own heart beat and felt fear turning to ice in one's veins. For of all the dread sensations of an earthquake, the worst is the feeling of indescribable horror which possesses one from head to foot, and which is neither excitement nor despair nor alarm, nor like anything one has ever known before. Only those who have felt it can comprehend it; it is the experience of a lifetime, bought in one single awful unearthly moment.

That third shock was the last of any severity, but lesser ones continued at intervals all the day and night following, and indeed for long thereafter. Scarcely anybody was brave enough when night came to venture again indoors. Some of our friends slept in the open gardens on benches or on mattresses spread upon the trembling ground; some slept in tents; some in the tiny bathing houses along the beach, and some, like gypsies, camped out in their own carriages. We were offered shelter by a friend whose villa, being at the east end of the town, was one of the few that had escaped injury, and there we all slept in the drawing-rooms on the ground floor, dressed and ready to rush into the garden at the first threatening of danger.

Our drive through the town to reach this villa, was like passing through some city of the dead. The deserted streets were blocked with débris from the mutilated, desolate, uninhabited and un-

A MENTONE VILLA AFTER THE EARTHQUAKE. (*From a photograph.*)

habitable houses. Here a wall was cracked open from top to botton; here cracked and seamed and blistered all over like a plate exposed to too great heat; here the whole front of a house had fallen out, and there a tower had come crashing down to the ground. Not a roof but had lost tiles and chimneys at least. Balustrades and balconies had given way on all sides. Windows were set awry. Shutters and doors hung flapping on broken hinges like helpless signals of distress. Great stones were twisted completely around as if they had spun like tops in their places, and plaster lay ash-like over everything, leaving great unsightly scar-like spots to mark from where it fell. It seemed an almost incredible transformation of the place. One felt as if the years had suddenly slipped back into the by-gone ages, and as if one were part and parcel oneself of some as yet unhistoried Herculaneum or Pompeii.

Thousands and thousands of people fled Northward that morning from all along the Riviera, many of them leaving bag and baggage behind them, for it is marvellous how quickly even one's dearest possessions lose all value the moment life is in peril. . . . . Six weeks since that terrible twenty-third of February, eighteen hundred and eighty-seven. Even the most timid and most unnerved have regained their courage and their lost spirits. Those whose houses were spared returned long since even into the upper storeys. The shops are reopened, and masons and bricklayers and carpenters are everywhere at work, repairing where repair is possible, and cheerily rebuilding where they must. The sentinels who forbade entrance at doors of condemned houses, and the soldiers who stood guard over streets unsafe for public traffic, have withdrawn their prohibitions and disappeared. Mentone will soon again wear its bright and smiling face of old. Yet while we live, none of us who were in the line of the earthquake, can ever forget that dim gray Ash Wednesday morning when we awoke so suddenly out of our Carnival dreams to find ourselves in sackcloth and ashes indeed, and with the *Miserere* stifled upon our lips.

A CATSKILL BEAR STORY.

"BEARS in the Catskills?"

Well, there certainly are none prowling about the Overlook Mountain House, nor the Hotel Kaaterskill, nor even in the vicinity of that romantic crag called Rip Van Winkle's Rock. In fact, during the week's ramble which we took — my friend and I — among the back woods and glens of Slide Mountain and the Indian Head, we failed to discover traces of either bear or wild-cat.

To say that we saw "neither hide nor hair" of them, as the phrase is, would not be true. There is a great, tawny, glass-eyed, stuffed wildcat at Meade's, on the Overlook; and in a farmer's house at Big Indian we saw a black bear's skin, the original wearer of which had been killed by the present owner, only a few winters ago.

But we found bear-stories — plenty of them. Whenever we met a native or old settler of the region, we straightway asked him for a bear-story; and he seldom disappointed us. We soon had quite a collection, the gem of which is the one I am going to tell you now. It has never before been told in print, I am sure; for we had it from the lips of the hero himself — an Italian laborer who, having originally come into the Catskills to work on one of the railroads, had finally made his home there.

Seated on a raft at the edge of the pond where we were fishing, he related his story in broken English, which I will endeavor to mend — not in the hope of making it funnier, but simply to render it more intelligible.

His name was Nanni (short for Giovanni) Rocco. It seems that in Italy, where Nanni was born and grew up, he had been a kind of showman. He used to travel among the Apennine villages with a performing bear, which he had taught to wrestle so skillfully that the huge animal, tightly muzzled and with claws blunted, would "throw" all comers who ventured to measure their strength with him. Then his master would try a bout, and always come off victorious; but this was due to a secret understanding with the bear, who, at a given signal, would fall to the ground and pretend to be overcome. This was done so naturally and so regularly, that after a while Nanni came to believe himself really more than a match for the beast; and the faithful creature never undeceived him.

The fame of Nanni and his wrestling bear spread far and wide. One day an agent came along and engaged him for a foreign tour, to extend as far as America. This began very successfully; and no doubt Nanni would have made his fortune in America, had not his indispensable partner, the bear, sickened and died shortly after their arrival in New York.

His master mourned him like a child. Such another animal was not to be found for love or money, and poor Nanni's occupation was gone. Disheartened and without resources, he finally engaged himself with a number of his fellow-countrymen, to work on the railroads. This employment, in the course of time, brought him to the Catskill Mountains.

When the line of the Ulster and Delaware Railroad was first surveyed, the region through which it passes had much more the air of a forest primeval than it possesses to-day. The principal "old settlers" then were the bears and panthers and wildcats, with here and there a rattlesnake. There was good sport in the mountains, at that period.

One day a good-sized bear, closely pursued by two hunters, came tearing through the underbrush, close by the place where Nanni and his companions were at work. It was a wild spot, overlooking that stupendous ravine where the snowy veil of the Kaaterskill Falls hangs gracefully down the black wall of wet rocks.

"Head him off!" cried the hunters.

But the Italian laborers were too frightened to dispute the passage of the panting animal. The mere sight of them, however, caused him to slacken his pace and look about him, his red tongue hang-

ON THE EDGE OF THE PRECIPICE.

ing out of his open mouth, and his mischievous little eyes flashing with rage and defiance.

Before him were the Italians, behind him the hunters. On one side was the precipice, and opposite stood Nanni — and *he* was not the man to run away.

If he trembled, it was from excitement and emotion — not from fear. The sight of the free, full-grown bear at bay, and rearing threateningly upon his hind-legs, caused a flood of recollections to rush through Nanni's mind. Inspired by the thought of his triumphant wrestling days, he had but one idea, and that was to get a good "side hold" of the bear, throw him on his back, and capture him.

"Stop-a! stop-a!" he screamed, motioning back the hunters, who had raised their guns to fire. "I'll catch-a him for you!"

To the speechless amazement of his comrades, he rushed forward and grappled with the infuriated bear, throwing one arm around the plump, hairy body, and with the other hand clutching the shaggy throat.

The struggle was terrific while it lasted, and by no means one-sided. Bruin snapped with his jaws, and slapped out wildly with his huge paws, tearing great strips from Nanni's clothing at each blow. He did not seem to be at all particular whether bits of Nanni's skin and flesh came with the cloth or not. Then the two fell, and rolled in the dust. The spectators cried:

"They'll go over, as sure as —"

Before the sentence was out of their mouths, crash! went man and bear over the precipice together. The others heard the crackling of branches as they fell and were lost to sight in the dense foliage that clothed the mountain-side.

Horror-stricken, the men scrambled down the rocks as best they could by roundabout ways, to pick up poor Nanni's mangled body.

Mangled indeed he was, when they found him, but not killed. He and the bear had providentially tumbled into a thicket of huckleberry-bushes on a ledge half-way down the ravine. Bruin had made off, leaving Nanni stunned, bleeding, and highly indignant.

"Dat-a bear no good-a," he said, in a feeble but protesting tone, to his rescuers. " He'not know-a how to wrestle. He not wrestle fair! "

This is not a fable, but it has a moral: Don't expect good behavior from others, according to your own ideas of proper conduct, when you pay no regard to theirs.

Margaret Sidney's Illustrated Quartos.

Golden West as Seen by the Ridgway Club.

4to, cloth, 2.25; boards, 1.75.

A pictorial and talkative run from Boston to Monterey for health and pleasure and information. And what the jolly party sees from the car windows is only part of the treat.

What the Seven Did, or the Doings of the Wordsworth Club.

4to, cloth, 2.25; boards, 1.75.

The seven are little girl neighbors, the Wordsworth Club, which met once a week at their several homes to have a good time. Those good times are the book. The best of them had to do with the fathers and mothers and Widow Barker's cow.

Who Told it to Me.

Square 8vo, boards, 1.25; cloth 1.75.

Neighbor boys and girls growing up together, having their ins and outs, and ups and downs; and the old folks had their share in the young folks' doings, as they ought. It was a jolly Pengannop. They did grow good men and women those days in New England.

Polly and the Children.

4to, boards, 50 cents.

The parrot has surprising adventures at the children's party and wears a medal after the fire.

Family Flight Series.

By E. E. HALE and SUSAN HALE, 5 vols., 8vo, boards, each, 1.75; cloth, 2.25.

Book journeys through the several countries with eyes and ears wide open, old eyes and young eyes and ears. The books are full of pictures, and fuller of knowledge not only of what is going on but what has gone on ever since book-making began, and fuller yet of brightness and interest. You see the old as old; but you see it; you see where it was and the marks it left. You see the new with eyes made sharper by knowledge of what has gone in the world.

In other words these books amount to something like going through these places with a traveling companion who knows all about them and their histories.

They are written and pictured for boys and girls; but there is nothing to hinder the old folks going along. Will you go?

FAMILY FLIGHT AROUND HOME.
FAMILY FLIGHT OVER EGYPT AND SYRIA.
FAMILY FLIGHT THROUGH FRANCE, GERMANY, NORWAY AND SWITZERLAND.
FAMILY FLIGHT THROUGH MEXICO.
FAMILY FLIGHT THROUGH SPAIN.

One of the most effective means of exciting and satisfying zeal for knowledge of the world we have in books.

All Among the Lighthouses, or the Cruise of the Goldenrod.

By MARY BRADFORD CROWNINSHIELD. 8vo, illustrated, cloth, 2.50.

Two boys and a girl accompany a government lighthouse inspector on his tour along the coast of Maine in the Steamship Goldenrod. They not only have the journey and see that remarkable coast; they have the lighthouse system explained with pictures and maps. A promising trip; and the book does it justice. Every inch of the way has its fill of delightful instruction.

The Ignoramuses.

By MARY BRADFORD CROWNINSHIELD. 8vo, illustrated, cloth, 2.50.

The same go to Europe. They not only had a good time themselves on the Goldenrod, but made a most entertaining book. So they go abroad for another. As before they go to learn; and, while they are about it, here's another book as good as the Lighthouse Cruise.

Dame Heraldry.

By F. S. W. Illustrated by nine pages of colored plates and numerous engravings. 8vo, cloth, 2.50.

The writer, his children having an interest in heraldry, set himself at the task of telling them what he knew of it. Hence the book; which treats the whole subject formally, yet with a pleasant vacation air.

Storied Holidays.

By ELBRIDGE S. BROOKS, author of The American Indian, In Leisler's Times, In No-Man's Land, and others. 12mo, cloth, $1.50.

An historic tale connected with a holiday in every month of the year.

There is the snapdragon Christmas quarrel of James I. of England with his sons about the release of Sir Walter Raleigh; a New Year's meeting of Margery More with Henry VIII; how William Penn got his motto " Be true, be leal, be constant," on St. Valentine's Day; how the Earl of Kildare kept St. Patrick's; the wise men of Gotham fool King John on the first of April; and so on through the months.

These stories out of history practise one in the times they take him back to.

A Midshipman at Large.

By CHARLES R. TALBOT. 12mo, cloth, $1.50.

An escapade of a bright young fellow who "shipped" for a yacthing cruise in vacation.

The story has nothing to do with the question whether it pays to know one's work and do it and "be," as the phrase goes, "a gentleman"; but, if the reader chooses to think of them, he will find plenty of stimulant.

www.ingramcontent.com/pod-product-compliance
Lightning Source LLC
Chambersburg PA
CBHW020259090426
42735CB00009B/1149